THE BIG BOOK OF BLOOMS

Botanical experts
Elisa Biondi and Scott Taylor
Royal Botanic Gardens, Kew

Blooms and wildlife expert
Barbara Taylor

Can you find ...
... the golden bulb hidden 15 times in
this book? Watch out for imposters...

THE BIG BOOK OF BLOOMS

Words and pictures by

YUVAL ZOMMER

In association with

Royal Botanic Gardens Kew

WHAT'S INSIDE

FLOWER FAMILIES

Do flowers have families?

They might not have brothers, sisters or parents, but all flowers are grouped into families based on the features they have in common, such as how they grow and what their flowers look like.

Bulb family

Tulips and lilies are from the same family. They grow from bulbs just like garlic, onions and daffodils!

Daisy family

Sunflowers, daisies, dandelions and marigolds are part of one of the largest plant families.

Prickly family

Plants in the cactus family have spines instead of leaves and can thrive in the driest environments on the planet.

Peapod family

The plants of sweet peas, chickpeas, peanuts and lentils have butterfly-like flowers made of five petals.

Orchid family

The orchid family has many colorful and fragrant blooms that grow worldwide.

Fruity family

Raspberries, apples and cherries are all part of one family, along with almonds and roses.

FLOWER ANATOMY

What are flowers for?

The main purpose of a flower is to help the plant it bloomed on to reproduce. The flower produces seeds that new plants grow from.

POLLEN

STIGMA

PETALS

STAMENS

SEPALS

BUD

Seed makers

To make seeds, a flower needs pollen from other flowers. Pollen is a fine powder created by a flower's stamens.

Pollen from one flower travels to another with the help of pollinators.

The pollen sticks to the stigma and begins the process of making seeds.

Support network

Sepals are the green outer parts of a flower. They protect young buds and support the petals.

Attention seekers

The petals are often bright and colorful to attract nectar-loving pollinators who play an important role in the seed-making process (see page 10).

Growing up

The stem grows up from the seed towards the sun, carrying water and nutrients to the rest of the plant.

ROOT SYSTEM

STEM

VEIN

Making a meal of it

Leaves take the energy from sunlight to make a sugary food, in a process called photosynthesis.

Strong foundations

Roots hold the plant in place so that it doesn't fall over. They absorb water and nutrients from the soil to help the plant grow.

POLLINATORS

What do pollinators do?

Pollinators such as bees, insects and birds do the important job of carrying pollen from one plant to another. The flower attracts them with a sugary food called nectar. The pollen sticks to their bodies when they stop to eat nectar, and then travels with them to the next plant they visit.

Night vision

Pale or white flowers are often pollinated by nocturnal insects like moths, which can easily see the plants in the dark.

Face facts

As bats lap up nectar from mango and banana plants, their furry faces become covered in pollen.

Tongue twisters

The long tongue of the sword-billed hummingbird is perfect for reaching the nectar inside tube-shaped flowers.

Champion pollinators

Hoverflies are one of the most important pollinators of fruit crops and wildflowers.

Shopping basket

Bees have a little hollow on their back legs, surrounded by hairs, to collect pollen and nectar.

COLORFUL FLOWERS

Why are roses red and violets blue?

Most flowers are brightly colored so that they stand out in a green garden or field and are easy for pollinators to see. Lines and patterns on a flower's petals help pollinators know where to land.

Bee-ing color blind

Bees can't see red but they can see blue, green and ultraviolet light, which is invisible to humans. They often visit blue and purple flowers.

Stop here!

The petals of the blue iris flower, with its yellow center, attract insects.

Nectar guides

The petals of the evening primrose flower have lines that guide moths to the nectar.

Big and bold

Bird pollinators are drawn to flamboyant, colorful flowers—especially red ones. Hummingbirds love red fuchsia flowers and tui birds in New Zealand adore flax flowers.

Landing zone

The center of the common toadflax flower is a bright yellow, making it stand out to bumblebees.

13

FLOWER POWER

What are flowers useful for?

Flowers attract pollinators using their bright colors or scents and produce new seeds. But over the years humans have discovered that flowers can do all sorts of other interesting things too.

Small but mighty

For decades the chemicals in the rosy periwinkle have been used in medicine to fight cancer.

Sip for strength!

Flowers like echinacea and hibiscus are brewed in teas to help people grow strong and healthy.

14

Achoooooo

Some flowers can heal, but others irritate human beings. Pollen from certain types of plants and trees, like ragweed and oak trees, can cause hay fever.

Ancient remedy

For thousands of years people have used lavender to soothe aching muscles. The Romans used to add the flowers to their baths.

VENUS FLYTRAPS

What's on the menu for a Venus flytrap?

This fearsome little plant is carnivorous and will eat not only flies, but also beetles, slugs, spiders and even tiny frogs, although ants are its favorite. Tasty!

The one and only

There is just one species of Venus flytrap, and it lurks in the subtropical wetlands on the East Coast of the U.S.

Going once, twice!

A trap can only open and close a few times before it dies and falls off. The plant will then grow a new trap from underground stems.

Make it snappy

With leaves that close like a clamshell this plant can snap itself shut and form a perfect trap.

Caught in a trap

When an insect brushes against more than two of the hairs on the inside of each leaf, it triggers the trap to snap shut in less than a second.

ROSES

Does your mummy like roses?

An ancient Egyptian mummy does! Rose wreaths from over 5,000 years ago have been found in ancient Egyptian tombs. People have been growing them ever since.

Thorny armor

Rose stems have sharp, hooked thorns to protect the plant from hungry animals who like to eat the flowers.

A pretty price

The world's most expensive rose is the Juliet rose. It took famous rose breeder David Austin 15 years and $3.7 million to develop this beautiful bloom.

$$$

Blast off!

Astronauts have grown a pink rose in space called "Overnight Scentsation." Without gravity, plant oils don't stay in the stem of a plant, so the flowers smell different from the same rose grown on Earth.

Thirsty work

Roses need up to 4 gallons of water to produce just one flower. That's over 50 cups!

PROTEAS

Are proteas really, really old?

Plants from this flowering family would have grown
alongside dinosaurs almost 90 million years ago.
More than 90 percent of proteas are only found
in one habitat in South Africa.

Sugar rush

Proteas are also known as sugarbushes,
because the flowers produce so much nectar.
Cape sugarbirds can't get enough of them.

Ready for lift-off!

The skyrocket protea's bright
yellow, deep orange or crimson
flowers look just like rockets
blasting into space.

Slowcoach

The snow protea is extremely rare. It only grows on two mountains in South Africa! After the first snow falls, the plant starts to open its flower very slowly—it takes a whole year!

Plant royalty

The king protea's open flower can be up to a foot wide—that's a pretty big buffet for its most frequent visitor, the Cape honeybee.

21

CHERRY BLOSSOMS

Why are they called cherry blossom trees?

Cherry blossom trees are named after their spectacular blooms and the fruit they produce. Some of the most famous cherry blossom trees are found in Japan.

Spring surprise

Cherry blossoms appear in spring, before the leaves come out on the trees. When the petals fall, they float softly down like snow, turning the ground pink or white.

Small but splendid

Most cherry blossom flowers are white or pink with five delicate little petals, but some have more than 20 petals.

Old and wise

Many cherry blossom trees will live for 50 years and some for as long as 100. The oldest tree is believed to be over 2,000 years old and grows at the Jissou Temple in Japan.

GIANT WATER LILIES

How big is a giant water lily?

These whoppers have flowers the size of a soccer ball. Their lily pads can grow over 6 feet wide and cover large areas in the Amazon River Basin.

A prickly personality

The red underside of the lily pad is covered in sharp spines. These protect the leaves from being nibbled by fish.

Perfumed prison

Every evening, the white flower of the giant water lily attracts beetles. When the insects crawl inside it, they become trapped!

Lily pad pool float

The pads of the giant water lily are full of tiny air pockets, which makes them buoyant enough to hold up to 55 pounds—that's the weight of a small child!

Birdie balancing act

Lily trotters are birds that have large feet and long toes, which makes it easy for them to walk around on the pads while they search for food.

Overnight, the flower turns pink and covers the beetles in pollen.

It then sets them free in the morning and they fly off to pollinate the next flower.

Leafy water tanks

A tank bromeliad collects water in the center of its leaves, which form a little bowl. The biggest plants can hold as much as 2 gallons of water.

Natural nurseries

Poison dart frogs keep their tadpoles safe in pools of rainwater that gather in a bromeliad's leaves, where they feed on algae and mosquito larvae.

SEEDS AND SEED DISPERSAL

How do seeds like to travel?

Seeds travel away from their parent plant to find their own
space, light, water and nutrients. They are transported by the
wind or water, or by hitching a ride on or inside animals (after
being eaten). Some plants even explode to scatter their seeds!

Stowaways

Burdock, cleavers and buttercups have
seeds with tiny hooks just like velcro,
which cling to animal fur.

Three, two, one. Fire!

Some plants like the flax flower have seed
pods that explode once they have dried out.

Fantastic flyers

Sycamore seeds spiral down from the tree, just like tiny helicopters. Dandelion and milkweed seeds are light and fluffy so that they can float in the wind.

Hitchhikers

Colorful fruit attracts hungry animals. For some fruits, being digested by an animal starts the seed's germination. The seeds come out in the animal's droppings, ready to grow.

DANGEROUS AND DEADLY

How do plants defend themselves?

Plants can't run away from their enemies, so sometimes they defend themselves from insects and bigger animals using chemical poisons. These poisons can be harmful to humans too!

Sweet poison

Oleander is one of the most poisonous plants in the world. Even eating honey made from oleander nectar could make you very sick.

Murderous plant

All parts of the deadly nightshade plant contain poison. It has been used to poison famous emperors, kings and warriors throughout history.

48

Pets beware!

Rhododendron flowers can be dangerous to small animals like cats and dogs, but the most toxic part of the plant is the nectar.

Hocus pocus crocus

The autumn crocus is a very unusual plant because its flowers emerge from the ground before the leaves. It contains a poison that can be deadly.

KEW GARDENERS

How do Kew gardeners help the world?

Did you know that Kew Gardens in London has the most diverse collection of living plants in the world? Botanists and scientists work together to grow and protect plants from all across the globe.

Learning and teaching

Scientists discover and identify new species of plants from all over the world and research the impact of climate change on habitats that are at risk.

Safekeeping

Endangered plants are grown and studied in plant nurseries to keep them safe and increase their numbers.

Adventure and discovery

Brave botanists travel across the world to study plants. They find new ones each year and keep observing them to check on their progress.

FLOWERS AND US

Do flowers have meanings?

For centuries, people have used blooms to send messages of love, friendship and sympathy.

Natural knowledge

For Buddhists, the lotus flower stands for spiritual wisdom and understanding. Buddhist artwork often uses lotus flowers to represent Buddha.

Happily ever after

In traditional Hindu weddings, fresh flower petals are sprinkled over the newlyweds as a blessing.